My Books

FICTION

Shards of Glass Series
Shards of Glass
Fragments of the Past
Memories Lost in Time

SHORT STORIES

One Summer

NON FICTION

How to Live with Bipolar
Bipolar 1 Disorder Rescue Plan
37 Symptoms of Bipolar Depression
The Bipolar Guide
A Practical Guide to Overcoming Loneliness

POETRY

We Never Did Mornings

HUMOUR

Funny Old Folk

FUNNY OLD FOLK

whimsical British humor

Sally Alter

INTRODUCTION

Aging is full of surprises, and none are more delightful than the odd little quirks that come with it. In Funny Old Folk, you'll meet a cast of characters who've fully embraced the peculiarities of getting older, and in doing so, have made their golden years a little brighter – and a whole lot stranger.

These stories aren't grand adventures or heartwarming life lessons. Instead, they're a playful wink at the odd, sometimes nonsensical realities of life past a certain age. Having spent her youth and early years in Britain, Sally Alter brought her absurdist English charm to the States. So, if you enjoy a bit of silliness with a dash of sharp British humor, you're in for a treat. And if you're offended by the idea of feeding 25 cats every morning or gleefully scanning the obituaries, well … perhaps these tales aren't for you.

But for everyone else, sit back, relax, and enjoy a laugh – or at least a knowing smile – at the wonderfully weird world of the funny old folk.

As a senior what do you think of internet dating? Is it a good way to meet people in retirement?

I am a senior and hadn't been on a date for years, so I thought, heh, what a great idea it would be to go on an internet dating site. So, I did just that.

First of all, the *'only $25.00 a month,'* is not deducted from your credit card once a month. Oh, no. You will find that six months of payments were swiped out of your account the moment you typed in your credit card number. You can't get that back if things go south. And worse, you find yourself on the old automatic roll-over system when your six months are up. Try getting out of that one.

The photographs people provide are usually about ten years old, so if you aren't fussy about looks, you are in luck. The best part is when you keep getting little red hearts and winking emojis on your computer screen. I used to rush home every day, switch on my computer, and wait with bated breath for all the little red hearts and winking emojis to pop up.

But, oh, dear, when you write to these men whose photos are ten years old, you suddenly find they have no interest whatsoever in getting to know you, all they want is sex. Obviously, they don't want to waste a lot of time if you are not a Brittney Spears look-alike.

Anyway, off I went on my first date, safety precautions strictly in place – my cell phone and my own transportation. If you are the nervous type, you would also be advised to take a Mace spray, a very loud whistle, and a hatchet should you get into hot water.

Guy number one:

There I was, on time, waiting patiently in the pre-arranged restaurant. *Hmm!* five minutes, ten minutes, then fifteen minutes later guy number one strolls in, cheerfully rubbing his hands together, huge smile from ear to ear. Personally, I am not keen on Hawaiian shirts, and this one was probably XXL and had flowery, neon motifs all over it. He bore no resemblance to his ten-year-old photo at all.

I thought the rubbing of hands together meant that an apology for being late was on its way, but see how wrong you can be. When he finally managed to edge his ample rear end into the seat opposite me in the booth, he took a deep breath and began his hour-long monologue of how wonderful he was and how he had been everywhere and done everything. After about ten minutes, I was nodding off and let my lunch go cold. Finally, up at the cash register, he glanced in my direction and said, *"Oh, your profile says you have traveled. Is that right?"* I paid for my meal and went home.

Guy number two:

I am quite reasonable when it comes to most things, but as you know by now tardiness is not something I suffer gladly, and guy number two was half an hour late, even worse than guy number one. I was sitting outside the restaurant, wondering how long I should wait when he rolled up.

"So sorry..." At least he was sorry, *"I got completely lost. Went to ... instead of ... then thought if I went round ... but when I went round ... I realized I was on the wrong road."* Me listening, nodding indulgently, my poor stomach growling.

When we went inside the restaurant, guy number two clapped his hand over his mouth and said, *"I have to apologize, I'm waiting for my new teeth to arrive. I thought they would ... but ... and now I have to ... but you don't mind, do you?"* Big toothless grin.

I could see that it was sad his new teeth hadn't arrived, but surely he should have rescheduled the date? Being toothless is not the best way to present yourself to a new person. But I am indulgent, so I indulged him.

Nice meal, I paid my share, then we went to his car. I decided (foolishly) that it couldn't be too bad going for a five-mile drive with a guy with no teeth. He was a non-smoker it said in his profile, and the fact that his car reeked of cigars was quite alarming. *"I air it out every night ... and only smoke the occasional cigar,"* he said. I rolled my eyes.

So, we went to a nearby lake, and twice around the ducks, he said, *"Er, would you ... would you like to come back to my place?"* What! I don't think so. He promptly drove me back to town and waved goodbye.

Guy number three:

If you think photos that are ten years old are bad, this guy's photo must have been of somebody else altogether. He was short, not tall, gray, not blond, and was perhaps the ugliest man I have ever strolled down the street with.

Even before we got to the restaurant, he began his monologue. I began to think *Mr. Hawaiian Shirt* and *Mr. Toothless Wonder* were quite good company compared to this guy. By the time we had our bargain plate of chicken wings down us, me covered from nose to chin in red hot sauce, I knew everything there is to know about dog training. I was shown all the doggie pictures he had on his cell phone and told about the impossible husky pup he had taught to 'Come,' and the wayward dachshund that he had got to 'Sit,' and the spotted great dane he had, single-handedly taught to walk in a straight line … yawn! yawn!

I finally got my money back from the online dating company and joined a nunnery.

What can I do when I'm bored in my house?

Oh, I never get bored because I always play the *Little People* game.

You may not have heard of that game, especially if you go to bed early, as it is then that the *Little People* usually come out to play.

I have a lot of *Little People* in my house. They gather in little groups to have a chat. I don't really know what they chat about because I can't hear what they say. I am a bit deaf.

Anyway, to stave off boredom I play the *Little People* game and take them one by one around the house and hide them. It takes me quite some time to do this because there are so many *Little People* and they are very good at hiding. Anyway, eventually I manage to get all the *Little People* into hiding places then I sit down and have a cup of tea.

After a while, I decide to go and find all the *Little People*. But that's when the game really gets good because I can't remember where I hid them. I know I put some in the bedroom but there is so much stuff in the bedroom these days that I sometimes have trouble finding where all the *Little People* are.

I look in all the other rooms of my house and see if I can find the *Little People*. Some rush out to frighten me, but they only make me laugh.

Eventually, I manage to find all the *Little People*, sit down and have another cup of tea.

Who gets bored? Not me!

Do old people start selling their belongings before they die realizing you can't take them with you to the afterlife?

I am no spring chicken, so I am making solid plans now for my funeral and my burial. I have a fascination with graveyards, and have spent my life visiting graveyards in England and other countries in Europe.

I really love doing rubbings of ancient head stones. I once lived in Cornwall in England and the church and graveyard in my village was 500 years old. I have some really interesting rubbings of these fascinating head stones. Some are so old they have all but disappeared into the earth.

Although some of the graveyards in America are nice, especially the Mexican ones that have jolly sayings on them, I am not sold on the idea of being buried in one of them.

I am a fan of Egyptian burials myself and have been to the New York museum several times to discuss this type of burial with the museum curator. He has allowed me, as a private guest, to come in at night when the museum is closed and take a special look to see how the Egyptians buried their dead. I usually take him some *homemade cookies* as a gesture of thanks.

I have been amazed, I don't mind telling you. Those Egyptians really knew what they were doing. They made their sarcophaguses to last, and their burial chambers are filled to the brim with gold and various items they will no doubt need in the afterlife. They even went to the afterlife with all their horses, and many essential kitchen supplies like mixers and rice cookers. Some even had their slaves buried with them.

Unfortunately, I don't have any horses to speak of, or slaves for that matter. I do have a lot of kitchen equipment that might be useful, though, so I shall get it all labeled and catalogued.

I have been to see the funeral director in town and he is more than willing to help me with my burial wishes. I have ordered a couple of *Egyptian Coptic jars to put my vital organs in* just in case I should need them in the afterlife.

My funeral will be rather expensive and the burial site will be out of this world. But I have a good credit score so the funeral director has given me a big fat loan that I can pay off before I depart this earth.

I have a very good dressmaker who works for the local theater company, so she is very experienced in making exquisite outfits for the stars. She is going to make me a gold, lame sheath dress with real rubies around the neck line. I will get her to sew my grandmother's pearls into the hem.

Unfortunately, I had a nasty shock when I took my grandmother's pearls to a pawn shop to be valued as I discovered they were made of plastic and paste, but never mind it is sentimental value that counts, don't you think?

Some people don't like the thought of dying at all, but I am very excited. I can't wait to be lowered into the burial plot that is being prepared for me. It is on top of a hill on the edge of town where I can get a good view of the river and watch all the kids jumping in the dam at the weekends.

It's a good idea to make yourself comfortable in the after-life, *that's my motto*, after all you might be there for the next 5,000 years.

Do people like food nowadays?

No, I'm afraid people no longer like food. It has gone out of fashion.

Once upon a time people couldn't get enough of the stuff. They used to cram their mouths full of sausages, burgers, fries, ice cream, any old thing they could get their hands on.

And when they ran out of handy food, they would go grovelling around in the forest sniffing out truffles before wild boar got their hoofs on them.

It was a terrible sight. Quite pathetic really. It was a wonder that people who sell food didn't get offended. I mean imagine grovelling around in the forest when pizzas are bubbling up in the oven.

But people like that, who would lower themselves enough to grovel around in the forest, get senile very quickly and lose touch with the fact that pizzas are next on the menu.

Nowadays, now that food is out of fashion, people like beer.

You can really get full on beer. People have known that for years. When you think of all the old taverns that were overflowing with mead, there was more than enough to go around.

Do you remember all the **pretty wenches** who served the mead in the **copper tankards**? They had a merry time of it, all dressed up in their little skimpy outfits swaying their child-bearing hips hither and thither. No wonder the people went to the taverns to get their beer.

Nowadays, beer is not so well thought of. All the taverns are closed and all the wenches have gone their merry way, and there is no mead to be had for a song and sixpence.

Do senior citizens find other senior citizens physically attractive?

I am over 70 and live in a retirement town, more's the pity, and it is chock-a-block full of widows and divorced women. Men are few and far between.

When I look at most of these *old geezers*, I don't find them at all attractive, quite the reverse. I see them shuffling around on their walkers, and I think, oh, no, *that's not for me*. I have been a care-giver all my life and don't need another person to care for, thank you very much. And that is what is usually on the menu with all these old men. Besides, they do not want women of my age. Oh, no, they are looking for swanky 21-year-olds who are plentiful if these men have a big fat bank balance, which many of them do in this town. We are not short on millionaires here.

I love living on my own and have no intention of being tied down again. I eat when I like and go out when I want. And there really isn't anything better than having complete control of the remote and the thermostat.

There is an activity center in my town which provides very reasonably priced four-course meals on week days. I have ventured in there a couple of times and ended up sitting on my own surrounded by little cliques of blue-haired women yacking about who-knows-what. Probably gossiping about the neighbors.

I once plonked myself down next to a pleasant looking guy and was surprised that he had a lot to say. He wasn't boring. We swapped notes on all kinds of things. He was an Anglophile and we had many laughs talking about all the British comedies. I was so taken with that conversation that when we left, I impulsively asked him if we could have lunch together another day. He almost jumped out of his shoes.

"Oh, no," he said, frowning at me as if I was a *psychedelic monster*. "I don't think my wife would like that."

I wasn't asking him to jump into bed with me. I only wanted a bit of conversation.

Once, a while back, I was invited to a party by one of the richest guys in town. He is president of this and that, and a big philanthropist for the arts. We met in a restaurant where I was dining with friends. I was at the desert bar (I always head for the deserts first before the entrees as their chocolate meringue pie is to die for) and there he was, *hair as white as salt*, 7' 8" tall, towering over me. I had no idea who he was, but didn't think a party would be any cause for alarm.

I dressed up to the nines in my brand new slinky black dress, backless no less, and hopped off in my impossibly high-heeled shoes to the party on my own. Guess what, nobody spoke to me at all. I stood at the buffet for about an hour, nibbling on the exquisite shrimp canapes, and bitterly regretted that I had gone to all that trouble to get dressed up. I could have been tucked up in my pj's at home, watching my mini-series on Netflix.

But there I was at this glamorous party that was given on a very grand scale, caterers and all, and brimming over with all the in-people in my town – mostly over 60 years old.

I wandered over to the balcony above *Mr. Rich guy*'s palatial great room and cast my eyes over all the guests who were swanning about on the plush Persian carpets below.

What do you know, *Mr. Rich guy* suddenly appeared beside me and asked me outright, "Are you married?"

I told him I was not, and that my husband died seven years ago. He hovered about for a bit, in silence, then departed.

I sipped on my Champagne and toyed with my ring. Then what do you know, ten minutes later, here comes Mr. Rich guy once again, hovering beside me.

"Did you say you've been widowed for seven years?"

I told him that was right, and thought he must have a screw loose, or something. More silence, more hovering, then another departure.

Well, I had had quite enough of that, so I swiped a nice fat chocolate eclair from the buffet, got in my car, and went home. What a relief it was to climb into my pj's and watch the next episode in my mini-series on Netflix.

So much for **_old geezers_** in this town. My slinky black dress hasn't been invited out of the closet since.

Do seniors pay more attention to their diet as they get older?

… I have a *very specialized diet.*

I only eat what looks good,

smells good,

and tastes good.

……If it looks like chocolate,

smells like chocolate,

and tastes like chocolate,

I eat it!

……I also like the smell

and the taste of key lime pie,

lemon meringue pie,

and pumpkin pie in season.

......When I see apple turnovers,

or cherry turnovers,

I buy them,

and eat them.

......I have a *very specialized diet*.

I only eat what I like

and leave the cardboard cheese

and jolly cakes

to all you dieters.

Do the elderly care about appearance?

I really don't know who the elderly are these days.

Does this elderlyness begin when you jog over to the fence in your yard in your 70s, or maybe when you stroll over to the fence in your 80s, or perhaps when you puff over to the fence in your 90s, or heaven forbid when you haven't got a leg to stand on and have to be dragged over to the fence in your 100s?

You know you are elderly by then because they chuck you into the **knacker's yard** and chop off your head. Make sure you don't make a fool of yourself by running around with your head still on the block.

Well, let's say I am an elderly 77 year old chicken, just for the hell of it.

So now that we have sorted that one out, on with your question. Do we the elderly *(me)* care about our *(my)* appearance?

Think long and hard about this one. Be honest. Be truthful now. Good God-fearing people are listening.

When I was a sassy young chic I was totally focused on my appearance. In fact, in my hay day, I had a swishy yard to go to in Oxford Street in London – the place to be – and trotted through the ginormous feed stores on my way to the yard every morning picking up all the best seed I could lay my claws on, arriving later weighed down with fancy seed bags that said John Lewis and Selfridges on them.

If my yard had been near Harrods, where the seed is exquisite to the taste, I would have had even fancier seed bags that said Harrods on them. You would really have seen the chicken cross the road then. I would have stopped traffic.

I suppose you could say I spent my life looking in the mirror. I was vain!

There I have said it. I admit it. I was vain.

Wonderful! When I was a young chick, I was admired most of time and really enjoyed myself. No harm done. Nobody suffered.

Many years have gone by in the yard since then with varying degrees of what mattered most about my appearance. I suppose it would be fair to say I always had my feathers fluffed, kept my cockscomb clean, and my sharp beak shiny.

Then, suddenly, I was an elderly hen – overnight it seemed.

My feathers went all stringy, and my pretty red cockscomb lay down flat. My skin turned sallow and prickly, my orange beak slipped, and my claws all fell out.

I rarely look in a mirror these days for fear I might see the real me – I happened to catch a glimpse of my reflection in a puddle yesterday and jumped back aghast. I had no idea I had wrinkles on top of the wrinkles I had last week. And they were on top of the wrinkles I had the week before that. Yet there they were, all wrinkly and crinkly and revolting.

My scraggy neck resembled the bottom of my chicken coup before its mucked out on Sundays.

I was a scarecrow, not a chicken. And I scared myself half to death.

So, I came to the conclusion that no amount of make up would ever cover up all those wrinkles and crinkles. This old bird was well and truly done for.

You can take me out and shoot me, then put me in a crock-pot with a sprig of parsley and have me for dinner.

Vanity rests with the young chicks around here. Elderly carcasses are good for **nothing but soup**.

How can I avoid wrinkles around my mouth when I get older?

If you are really serious about preventing wrinkles around your mouth when you get older, there are several things you can do. Some take a bit more dedication that others, but if you can do just a few of them, you might never see a wrinkle appear around your mouth - even if you live to 105.

The way you engage with other people can play a huge part in your long-term success. You never want to be seen in groups or in twosomes. Being around other people is far too risky - you might get carried away in conversation and lose sight of your goal altogether.

If you are serious about what you want to achieve it is far better, and easier, if you spend the rest of your life alone and in silence.

You could become a *nun*, or one of those amazing characters in loin cloths who sit in the Himalayas contemplating their navel. In your case, though, you would definitely need to avoid squinting into the sun.

The weather, the beach, the trampoline in your back yard are all disaster zones. And remember that diet and sleep, though good for others, must be avoided altogether if you want to avoid wrinkles around your mouth.

Here are just a few things that may help:

o   Stop smiling

o   Stop laughing

o   Stop pouting

o   *Stop talking*

o   Stop tensing your jaw

o   Never open your mouth wider than the size of
     a marshmallow

o   Never exclaim out loud if something shocks you rigid

o   Tape your mouth shut if you can't resist sleeping

o   Never gulp down your food if you can't resist eating

o   *Never drink water*

o   Always remember to gargle with your mouth shut

o   Never floss

o   Never go to the dentist

o   And most of all, never ride a bicycle down a hill or
     you might scream like a kid in first grade

The only problem with these suggestions is that you would need to start practicing in your youth for them to be 100% effective. Never mind, if you get rich quick you can afford plastic surgery on the wrinkles around your mouth.

How does moving around a lot affect a person?

Well I always think that people who fidget a lot are suffering badly from *hemorrhoids*.

It is a very sad tale indeed, but many millions of people suffer from *hemorrhoids*. In fact the company that makes *hemorrhoid* cream is making loot hand over fist out of all these *hemorrhoidal* people.

Hemorrhoids are caused by straining. If you find it necessary to sit on the toilet for hours at a time, straining and wheezing, then you have a problem.

It is not natural to have to pant and moan on the toilet. How do you think the poor toilet seat feels? It is bad enough supporting your weight without sweating all over it and causing it pain. Toilet seats suffer badly from pain.

But, no, fidgeting around a lot really does affect a person. These hemorrhoidal people have a dreadful time sitting at bus shelters, or sitting in trains, or even sitting in cars.

Their sitting mechanisms are all rusty due to sitting badly, all to one side, to avoid pain in their *hemorrhoids*.

The answer is coffee.

Chocolate is good. And so are bananas, but coffee is the Queen when it comes to *hemorrhoidal* discomfort. If you have your hot morning beverage on the toilet (pray for the seat) you will find that it is a piece of cake to go.

Then you can avoid *hemorrhoids* altogether.

How long should seniors date before marriage?

Seniors should never date before marriage.

Imagine if all the old people were courting at the same time, the place would be littered with old people doing their thing. You wouldn't be able to move about freely. It is unthinkable.

I can just see the place totally overcrowded with old people taking up all the seats in the cinema and grabbing all the tables in the restaurants. You wouldn't be able to see your favorite movie, and would probably die of hunger.

And never mind about going to the zoo. You would be jostled about in the queue and not be able to get to the kiosk because all the old people would be flashing their Social Security cards and demanding half price admission.

Old people are terrible dancers, as well, yet if they were dating there would be old people cluttering up all the dance floors in the nation, shaking their booty. There would be no elbow room, no place for you to get your kicks.

Nobody wants to see ***throngs of old people*** strolling about in the towns looking for other old people to date. It would be hard to cross the road because they would be all clogged up with herds of old people loitering about at all hours of the day and night.

They would have to employ more police men to round them all up and move them along.

No, old people ***should be seen and not heard***, like children.

They shouldn't be allowed to date at all. They should get married the moment they meet, and hide themselves behind closed doors.

Is it better to be old or young?

What a silly question.

Of course, being old is better than being young. When you are young you are tied down with a mortgage, screaming kids, and college debt.

How awful is that?

When you are old (over 70) life begins to take on a new meaning. You are free to do exactly what you like.

Here's just a few things you can do without getting arrested:

o   You can take your great dane guide dog on the plane.

o   You can sunbathe in the nude because *nobody will notice*.

o   You can even go to parties in the nude because *nobody will notice that either*.

o   You can drink all you like at parties and be sure that somebody will pay your taxi fare home.

o   You can eat desert first at all the best restaurants.

o   You can take out your teeth and give them an airing on the restaurant table.

o   You can twiddle with your hearing aid and listen in to juicy conversations.

o   And when somebody asks if you've got your hearing aid switched on you can say, "No, I'm saving on batteries."

o   You can join a singles club, and be thankful you're still single.

o   You can try meals on wheels, and be thankful you can still boil eggs.

o   You can park on double yellow lines and say, "Sorry, I didn't see them."

o   You can even drive through store windows, look innocent, and say, "Sorry, I thought the accelerator was the brake."

o   You can read the **obituary column** every morning and be thankful you're not in it.

o   You can make frequent visits to the cemetery and be glad you're not living there either.

o   You can choose your ideal weight and write it in large numbers on the scale where you can see it.

o   You can go to Disney World and get in half price.

o   You can send yourself a love letter, and sign it **Brad Pitt**.

Is it fun to live in senior housing?

Of course, it's fun to live in senior housing. Why else would people who live there always be smiling?

It's not because of the food. They don't eat the food, they eat out, but it's fun to live in senior housing because of all the nice people you have to talk to every day.

There's *Mrs. Loudwinkle* in No. 10. She's very nice, but you have to catch her on the run because she is always in the bathroom. I have no idea what she gets up to in there, but I always talk to her in between bathroom trips. She is very nice.

Then there's old *Joe Wigginsthrop* in No. 6. He's very nice, not as nice as *Mrs. Loudwinkle*, but he hasn't been here very long either. You get nicer the longer you stay here. That's a fact. There's something in the water, I think. Whatever it is, I love it. I drink lots of water like they tell us to and I meet the nicest people.

Mrs. Codswallop from No. 9 is very nice as well, but she's half crazy. Not whole crazy. That would be too much, even for me. But when she is half crazy she is very nice. I like her a lot, but I am very careful not to drink as much water as she does. I don't want to be half crazy. She is in the bathroom with *Mrs. Loudwinkle* from No. 10 all the time.

I have no idea what they get up to in there, but they are very nice when they are not in the bathroom.

I would say to any new residents, "Drink as much water as you possibly can. You will find the people are very nice in here. But don't drink as much water as Mrs. Codswallop from No. 9 because she is half-crazy."

When you are passing, drop in and have a glass of water. It is very nice.

Should old people read books?

No, old people should never read books of any kind.

If old people were to read books they might be influenced by them and be tempted to do something really stupid.

Imagine an old person reading a book on deep sea diving, for example. They might go out at night in a boat, jump into the sea and drown. The problem is old people get easily distracted. If they had finished the book and learned how to do deep sea diving in a sensible manner, they might not do something stupid and drown.

And what about a book on bird watching in the mountains. That would be a disaster if an old person was tempted to climb up a mountain in their sensible shoes just to see a stupid bird. And how would they be able to hold on to their glasses and their binoculars, and the bird book, and their sandwiches, and the mountain peak at the same time? They might do something really stupid and fall down.

If old people were to read books about skinny dipping that would be really stupid. Imagine how the fish would feel when they saw a wrinkly old person jumping into the lake in their birthday suit. It might give the fish a heart attack. Or indigestion, at the very least. Fish shouldn't have to endure such sights when they are minding their own business swimming round and round in the lake.

It is imperative that books of any kind should be kept well hidden from all old people because they might be tempted to do something really stupid.

They don't have the sense when they are old to sit down in a chair and read a book without being distracted. They get tempted to do all kinds of stupid things and expect the rest of us to rescue them.

No, *old people should never read books* of any kind.

What are some positive things about dying?

Dying is great!

o   You don't have to get up early in the morning to go to work.

o   You don't have to tolerate your toxic relatives.

o   You don't even have to remember their birthdays.

o   You can lie back in peace and leave all the funeral arrangements to some hapless individual who has been unlucky enough to outlive you.

o   You don't even have to pay for the funeral.

o   You don't have to wear black.

o   If you are really lucky, and they bury you way out of town, you don't have to put up with your toxic relatives coming over to bug you.

o   You never have to pay the mortgage again. And you can send wicked thoughts to the bank manager who gave you such a hard time getting it in the first place.

o   You are no longer expected to be nice and kind and thoughtful to everybody.

o   You can *fart as much as you like*.

Dying is great! You don't even have to look in the obituaries anymore to see if your name is in it.

What are some ways for a 70 year-old to stay hip?

Well that's pretty easy these days.

You can go to the thrift store and buy the most wonderful outfits like butt-hugging denim shorts with holes in strategic places and fringed legs. Then, if you are lucky, you might find a nice, red sequined bolero and wear that to the supermarket. That makes a nice *hip* outfit.

You can also get some really great shoes at the thrift store. How about some nice gold, pointy-toe shoes with 7" heels? They often have high-heeled cowboy boots in alligator leather as well at the thrift shop. You would look just great in them, and would be quite the thing on the dance floor.

Cars are a great way to stay *hip*. If you've got a boring old Camry or Ford Fusion, trade it in and get an old jalopy Jeep, or even a rust bucket. You can make a great impression driving around in your rust bucket with the roof down. You could even put a few American flags on the top and let them flap around in the breeze when you career through town at 99 mph.

How about taking a stroll through the local park, sporting your new boom box. You don't have to worry about how loud it is playing because you won't be able to hear it anyway. Just think what fun it would be for the ducks. Make a nice change from a loaf of white bread. If the police bear down on you, you can say, *"I'm employed by park management to entertain the wildlife."*

You can also take a tasty picnic lunch to the park and make all the young folk drool when you take out your bucket of 44 Dairy Queen chicken nuggets and your 15 milkshakes. When you are *hip*, you don't just buy one boring old vanilla milk shake, you can have a whole collection of every single milk shake that Dairy Queen makes. Line them all up on the picnic table and grin roguishly at the kids.

Oh, and just think what fun you can have with the neighbors when you are *hip*. You can build a 25 foot tall sand castle in the middle of the yard and stick strobe lights and bull horns all over it. When the neighbors scream at you to put the lights out and cut out the noise, you can say, "I'm watching for bats."

Now, I'm sure you can see the joys of being *hip* at the age of 70, but now you've got to think about what to do when you are 71.

What are the ten most important things one needs to know about being over sixty?

I am now in my 70s, so trying to remember back to being a 'spring chicken' of 60 may be a little difficult, but here are the most important things one needs to know about being over sixty:

1. You can say anything you like because *nobody listens* to you anyway.

2. You suddenly find that hairdressers have no idea what to do with your hair.

3. You also find that there is no such thing as fashion for the over 60s.

4. No matter how you do your make up you *still look a mess*.

5. You look in the mirror and, as you suspected, you are just not there.

6. You should go to parties naked because that's the only way you will be noticed.

7. You suddenly realize that when they said save your money for retirement, they were right.

8. It seems absurd to call police men, "Sir," because they all look like little boys.

9. Doctors are always delighted to see you. They rub their hands together with glee.

10. No matter how much you have exercised and dieted everything goes South.

What conversations only exist between old people?

That's an easy one. After the age of 65 conversations between people are about health, or rather lack of it.

This is when everything seems to break down, go south, or fall apart, and there are so many people around you who are experiencing the same things. it's just great to share all your problems with them.

A typical conversation between a 65-year-old woman and a 68-year-old woman:

First person: "How are you feeling?"

Second person: "Oh, my knees are killing me. This arthritis is so bad I can barely get about these days. I have to keep sitting down to rest my poor old legs."

First person jumps in: "Oh, you have no idea how bad my back is. The doctor says there's nothing wrong with it, and even the x-rays don't show much, but I can tell you I can hardly get out of bed ..."

Second person can't wait to weigh in: "Oh, I know exactly what you mean ..." quick pause for breath. "My back was bad like that for years. I had to have it operated on to get ..."

First person: "I'm not going through no operations. Oh, dear me, no. I don't trust those doctors with ..."

Second person: "You shouldn't worry about that. They are really good, I can recommend ..."

First person: "Nothing would convince me to go under the knife."

Second person: "Well, it's good to see you. I'm off to the doctor's now so I can't stop."

I am 77, so I know what I am talking about, more's the pity.

What do gorgeous people do when they lose their social advantages due to loss of attractiveness?

I am old but still gorgeous. I look in the mirror every day and congratulate myself on my goreousness. I don't notice my wrinkles

All the social advantages are still lying at my feet. I walk on a red carpet wherever I go. Lilies are tossed down in front of me. *People swoon*.

So where did you get the idea that attractiveness dies with old age, and that people have to give in to a life of gloom and disaster?

There is so much drudgery and tragedy in this world right now, why not feel as gorgeous as you like. It won't kill you. It will make you feel young and lovely again.

I love that feeling. I am bubbling over like a tall glass of Champagne.

I am in my 70s with a lot of pain, but, *heh*, I got up just now and waltzed around the room to the wonderful vibes of the Vienna Philharmonic. Would you deny me that, just because I am old?

It's a shame my attractiveness has gone down the toilet. But I can dream

What do old people do to pass time?

I am 77 and live on my own, so I have a lot of spare time.

Here are some of the things I do to pass the time:

o   On *Sundays* I spend an inordinate amount of time sitting on the bathroom floor contemplating my navel.

o   On *Mondays* I go to the Activity Center in town and spend a very happy hour laughing uproariously at all the old ladies trying to do square dancing.

o   On *Tuesdays* I do the laundry. I wash all the clothes I have worn in the house during the past week, the clothes I wore to the Activity Center, the clothes I wore to do the grocery shopping, the pillows, the comforters, the tea towels, the towels, the table cloths, the curtains, the cushions, the face flannels, the dish cloths, the handkerchiefs, the dressing gowns, and the blankets.

- o   On *Wednesdays* I iron all the clothes I have worn in the house during the past week, the clothes I wore to the Activity Center, the clothes I wore to the grocery store, the pillows, the comforters, the tea towels, the towels, the table clothes, the curtains, the cushions, the face flannels, the dish cloths, the handkerchiefs, the dressing gowns, and the blankets.

- o   On *Thursdays* I clean the range, the dishwasher, the fridge, the washing machine, the dryer, the toaster, the microwave, the electric hood, the food processor, the blender, the kitchen counter tops, the fronts of the cupboards and drawers.

- o   On *Fridays* I clean the kitchen floor, the bathroom floor, the other bathroom floor, the studio floor, the first bedroom floor, the second bedroom floor, the hall floor, the garage floor and the shed floor. I also sweep the deck at the front of the house, the deck at the back of the house, and the garden path.

- o   On *Saturdays* I do all my grocery shopping, then I go to I Hop and have 3 eggs, 3 sausages, 3 hash browns, 3 pancakes, 3 muffins, 3 pieces of French toast, a large banana boat covered in nuts, cream, chocolate and strawberry sauce, with strawberries on top.

It's hard to fill up the days because I have so much time to spare, but I do my best.

What do old people need to live actively?

I don't know what you mean by old people, but assuming you are very young, old can be anybody over the age of 45, I suppose.

Seeing as I am in my 70s, I imagine I am really over the hill, and according to society, the medical profession, fashionable magazines, TV talk shows, sports enthusiasts, mental health experts, sports equipment and apparel manufacturers, I should be out there pounding the pavements in my Niki's.

I hate exercise.

I have joined three gyms, mostly at the urging of others, paid out all manner of ghastly fees and wasted my money. Oh, I do make an appearance for a couple of weeks. I do try hard to do my rounds on the treadmill, the exercise bikes, the weights but – yawn!, yawn!– I find it, oh, so boring.

Gyms are incredibly fearful places – all I see when I enter are rows and rows of iron men, larger than life robots on the face of the moon- gyms resemble torture chambers to me. And who in their right mind would want to submit themselves to torture all in the name of good health?

No, it is the good life of the ***couch-potato*** for me.

I rock here all day in my trusty recliner, happily typing away on Quora, and stuffing myself silly with pastries and chocolates in the afternoon, then Brie cheese and crackers and a nice glass of Pino after the news at 6. At 7 I climb into my PJs and relax to a couple of hours of You Tube videos, or a ***nice juicy murder*** on Netflix.

Yes, my bottom gets numb, and I am in very poor shape indeed. My hips hurt, my knee creaks, and my eyes are watering by the end of the day, but how I love my cushy couch-potato life style, casually watching all the joggers puffing past my window, sweat dripping off their noses.

Not for me. I live the life of Riley, and shall almost certainly pay the price when I am really old. They'll have to put me out to pasture then.

What do senior citizens miss in their daily lives?

I don't miss much because I am good at reinventing sliced bread.

But I do miss the following, or some of them:

o   My 25 cats all *barking* at once

o   My scarlet dress that danced on its own at raucous parties

o   My house in the Bahamas where it never stopped snowing

o   Also my house in the Outer Hebrides which is Outer this World

o   My singing voice before a frog moved into my throat

o   All my friends who got on my nerves – 7 days a week

o   Walking on water at 3 in the morning

o   Walking upside down at 5

o   Knitting cross stitch through pages

o   Watching finless fishes fall in the stream

o   I really miss a good old belly laugh

o   And the joy of being silly

What does a normal 68 year-old living alone do? Is it normal for them to sleep a lot and not do much?

Yes, it's quite normal to sleep a lot and not do much when you are 68 years old. It is called hibernation.

Us old folk love to hibernate and do nothing – it's what you do when your life is winding down to a close. Ah, just let me curl up in a little ball and stay nice and warm in my little hole.

I spend a lot of time in my dressing gown. I love my dressing gown because it is nice and warm. I wear it when I am curled up in a little ball. I stay nice and warm in my little hole.

This dressing gown has seen me through several periods of hibernation.

When the winter's gone and the sun comes up over the hill, you will see all of us old folk climbing out of our little holes and neatly folding our dressing gowns up until the next winter.

There is nothing quite like the hibernation period. You can do absolutely nothing but sleep, like a little bear in a little hole. A little bear in a dressing gown in a little hole. Hibernating.

Just you wait until you are old, then you will be able to sleep all day and do nothing. You will be able to get into your dressing gown and curl up in a little ball in your cozy little hole. You can sleep all day, and nobody will bother you.

That's what us old folk do.

What does the queen do when she's on a long drive and needs to use the loo?

This question does not apply to British Royalty. *Our dear Queen*, in all her wisdom, had a complete bladderectomy when she first sat on the throne, and has never looked back since.

This is the operation of choice. It has the Royal stamp of approval.

A bladderectomy may be a little uncomfortable at first, but being without a bladder is no hardship at all. It is quite amazing how much time can be saved by not having to pop off to the loo every time you have a cup of tea.

In the Queen's case, she is completely free to ride horses for ten hours at a time without ever having to worry about *squatting behind a bush* in the willy wilds. She can also safely do heroic jumps on her horse without fear of post-menopausal leaks. It is quite a boon.

If you were to ask the Queen, I am quite sure she would recommend a bladderectomy to even her lowliest subjects.

She would say:

"My Husband and I are great proponents of bladder-ectomies, and can attest to being fancy-free, nappy-free, diaper-free, and Depends-free for years. We love it."

Of course, everyday, mere mortals, who can't afford private care have to wait about 20 years for a coveted bladder-ectomy on the NHS.

But, oh, my, it's worth it.

What have you grown to accept as you've gotten older?

My life is better now that I am old -

…………I have dumped all my mirrors,

…………wear long, hooded robes,

…………and never leave the house.

I can eat all I want -

…………because long, hooded robes are voluminous,

…………don't shrink in the wash,

…………and don't show food stains down the front.

I find that living alone is great -

…………I wish I had done it years ago,

…………preferably when I was still married

…………to my various pitiful husbands.

My choices were iffy at best when it came to *husbands* -

…………and *friends*,

…………and *lovers*,

…………...and *hairdressers*.

I no longer care about my hair -

…………hoods hide a multitude of sins,

…………Buddhists are bald,

…………and I am much better at choosing religions
        than hairdressers or husbands.

I find that friends are great if they never write -

…………or phone,

…………and live in another country entirely.

…………That also goes for *husbands*.

What is a typical day like for a person who is 65 or older?

As I am now in my 70s, my typical day starts at around 10 or 11 in the morning. I am not a morning person. By that time my cats (all 25 of them) are standing cross-legged at the bottom of the bed, yowling. They are waiting for me to get up and change their litter boxes.

Some of my cats get so fed up with waiting they change it themselves which saves me a lot of bother. It is so nice to have *helpful cats*.

But first I have to take my tablet because if I don't take the first tablet that is a thyroid tablet that has to be taken at least an hour before I eat, I forget about taking all the other 15 tablets when I am supposed to take them, besides it often gets so late in the day that I forget to take them altogether, and so much time passes that I end up taking them at night when I am supposed to take my night time tablets in order to get to sleep again.

It is a bit complicated – and I haven't fed the cats yet.

Feeding the cats takes some time, and their morning meal usually ends up being their evening meal. It is very time-consuming feeding 25 cats.

After I eat my bar of Hershey's milk chocolate with almonds, I am all set for the day.

Now I can relax with my jig saw puzzles and keep myself to myself. I am absolutely addicted to jig saw puzzles and do them while watching the news on TV at night. I don't answer the phone while the news is on and certainly don't entertain visitors.

I have to say, though, last night was different. The woman from the cattery turned up, unannounced, just when I was in the middle of my jig saw puzzle, and the news was about to start. I was miffed, to say the least. I told her I was going to be very rude and watch the news, and if she could wait, I would be free to talk to her at 7 o'clock.

She was a bit of a bother though because she wanted to inspect my house to see if my cats were being taken care of even though I have sent her many photos in the past, and had her round more than once before. She is very nosy.

By the time my jig saw puzzle and the news were finished, the lady from the cattery had done with her inspection and gave me a ***Certificate of Cat Happiness*** to put on the shelf along with all my other certificates of past years because I am always kind to my cats.

I can't write much more about my day because the lady from the cattery got me so wound up last night that I can't stop thinking of her and how nosy she is. She really is a bit of a bother.

I shall do a few jigsaw puzzles now and wait for the news.

What is the worst thing you can do when you are a senior?

When you arc a senior, the worst thing you can do is lie.

Seniors are far more prone to lying than most people. In fact they are prone half the time because they are always lying. I think they call it The Resting Pose in yoga. But any rate it is lying, isn't it?

Lying is out. It is OK to stand up, or even to walk around, but lying won't do at all. When you lie around all day you get complacent. You start thinking that you can just lie in bed and let the world rush around taking care of you.

Well, I am here to tell you that I never lie. I hate lying.

I always stand up or walk about. Oh, actually, come to think of it, I do sit around a lot but that's not strictly lying, is it? When you sit down your feet are still on the ground.

People in geriatric wards are always lying. When they no longer sit or stand, nurses say they are 'off their legs.' Can you imagine. That spells a life of lying to me.

"Oh, Mrs. Johnson, don't take any notice of her," says one nurse to the other. *"She's always lying. She's off her legs."*

When you are off your legs, before you know it you will be lying. In fact, you no longer sit or stand, and you definitely don't walk about, you just lie around all day and never think about your legs.

Well, I am here to tell you that I think about my legs a lot. I love my legs. I am not lying when I say that. I have lovely legs. I'm not about to go off them any time soon.

And I am not lying.

What meds do old people take?

Well, I'm 77 and take an awful lot of medicines, I think. I share them, generously, with the cat. The inside cat that is. The outside cat doesn't need any medicines as he sleeps in the rain. *Rain is very good for cats, it keeps them occupied.*

Oh, you were talking about people, weren't you, not wet cats?

Now let's see. What medicines do I take?

Well, the very first pill I take in the morning a hugehello-fapinkhorsesizedpill – is my worming tablet. Oh, no, sorry, ha ha, I give that pill to the cat. No, not the horse, silly, I don't have a horse, but if I did have a horse, I would give it ten hundred horse pills because if you work it out in pounds, and think of *horses as bigger than cats*, even wet cats, then you will have to ... Oh! No! forgot what I was saying. That's what happens when you are 77.

Anyway, back to my pills. I think pills are really goooooood for you. *(Sorry about that, my typing finger slipped again).* Anyone who doesn't take pills is either senile or lying.

I knew a woman once, a really nice woman, who boasted to me that she had never taken a pill in her life, even a vitamin C, then the very next week she slipped on a banana skin and died. I tell you, you are much safer on your feet if you take vitamin C.

I just can't seem to get back to my pills, can I? That's what happens in old age. I have to rely on my cat, not my wet cat, my inside cat to bark at me a few times to remind me to take my pills in the morning, I think. *This cat lives on a race track*, you'd better believe it, and is always skidding round corners from room to room in my house. She seems to have an aversion to keeping still.

She is such a squirmy cat that whenever I have to give her her worming pill, I have to yank her off the race track, wrestle her to the ground and *shove the pill up her bum*. No, not the horse, silly. I don't have a horse, remember? And if I did have a horse I would have to climb up on a step ladder to get to its bum, wouldn't I? and I am not about to do that as I got a very nasty letter from the ER department once telling me, in no uncertain terms, not to call in again until I break a finger nail, or something silly like that.

Oh, back to the cat, not the horse, and giving her her huge-hellofapinkhorsesizedpill up her bum. Believe me, that's the only way you can give a pill to a *racing cat*.

Me - oh, no, I don't take any pills, I think.

At 77 you can be as silly as you like.

What should every elderly person have on their wish list?

All the things young people have on their wish lists.

But they have to put *Urgent* in case they die before they get them!

What three things should a person avoid when they are past 70?

I don't know what men over 70 should avoid, so I can only speak as a 77 year-old woman. Bear with me.

The first thing to avoid is parties.

Avoid parties at all costs. It doesn't matter what kind of party you are invited to, or who you should be trying to impress, if you accept the invitation and go to a party, you will live to regret it.

o   You will be completely stuck when it comes to what to wear. Your wardrobe that's now filled with flowery, long sleeved shirts that cover your wobbly arms, far-too-tight polyester pants that ride up your bum when you walk, and silly, peaked caps in various renderings of red, white, and blue are just not suitable to wear at parties. And none of your 20 pairs of sensible shoes will look good with anything.

o   Don't even think about what to do with your hair. Now that you can see your scalp shining through your thinning gray bob, and it is not long enough to hide your turkey neck or to cover your multi-lined cleavage it is just a no-hoper.

o   Make-up, as you know by now, is a disastrous forgone conclusion. It just will not work. If you don't wear any you will disappear into the woodwork, and if you do have the guts to deck yourself out in your gold, sparkling eye shadow and your new red blush, you will only look like Rudolph the Red Nose Reindeer and be put to work to keep the kids happy. So, parties are out.

The second thing to avoid is kids.

o   Kids of all descriptions are no longer good for the constitution.

o   Even though they may be your own grand-kids, and even if they are the nicest kids on the block, they will be constantly at you. "Grandma, come and play on the swings with me." Or, "Grandma, come and play a video game with me." Or "Grandma, come and play electric trains."

o   First of all, you will want to take your nap. *Nobody disturbs your nap*. And secondly, you will not be able to get your bum in between the handles of the swings, you will not be able to make head nor tail of a video game – what are they anyway? And if you are foolish enough to get down on the floor to play with electric trains, they will have to hire a crane to get you up. No, kids are definitely out.

The third thing to avoid is holidays.

o   If you think in your wildest dreams that you will be able to enjoy a road trip, think again. Do you really want to be sweating for 10 hours in 90-degree heat in traffic jams, or maybe trying to read a road map with your bifocals sliding down your nose in the heat, or your unreliable bladder suffering in silence between rest areas? I think not.

o   And Disney World with the kids? OMG! Do you really want to stand in wavy lines that double back on each other, then double back on each other again, then double back ….? Or slump around, sweat dripping off your chin, holding your cotton candy. Or all but lose consciousness on the big dipper rides? I don't think so.

o   And if you think it would be nice to visit *Aunty Maud* in Australia, brace yourself. When they say you will be in coach don't imagine you will be able to get out and stretch your legs to avoid a blood clot. Or that you will be able to lie back in your seat without your chair ending up in somebody's dinner. Or that you won't be totally comatose for two days with jet lag when you get there. Plane trips to Australia, or even to Hawaii, are a disaster waiting to happen. Holidays of all descriptions are definitely out.

So now that you have decided not to go to parties, not to have anything to do with kids, and not to even think about leaving home, what's left?

That's a silly question – you just grab your old man by the pants, of course, and drag him upstairs to make hay while the sun shines.

What topics do old people talk about?

I can assure you, having recently joined the *Old People's Club*, that most old people talk about health and health care.

All day.

Or perhaps I should say sickness and Wealth Care! That makes more sense.

Whatever you want to call it, you can be sure that old people are adept at holding long-winded monologues about their arthritis, their heart attacks, their gall bladders, their back aches, even how many medications they take a day.

It has become quite a common old folk's competition to see who takes the most medications, and what they are for.

*"I take **62 pills** a day,"* says one old person with a sigh. *"Plus, another **34 vitamins**."*

Then the second old person says, *"Oh, I take far more than you do. I take **75 pills** a day now that my doctor has given me another **6 for my indigestion**. I can't afford any vitamins."*

"Well," says another old person. *"Mrs. Brown up the road takes **82 pills** every day. She's got bad **hemorrhoids**."*

To which they all sigh, *"Ain't it awful?"*

Then of course, we can't forget all the procedures and operations. There's the lumps on their foreheads, the mammograms, **colonoscopies**, polyps, hospital stays for hip replacements, nausea, vertigo, even long courses of physical therapy that seem to go on forever to help them recover from their latest knee replacement.

It is absolutely fascinating.

But I have to admit to you, on the sly, I am guilty of the very same thing. I love to talk about how many medications I take (join the competition) and all the procedures I am presently undergoing (spinal epidural this week, two MRIs last week). And of course, I don't forget to mention all the hospital stays I have had in the past two years and what they were all for.

I have become a very active member of the *Old People's Club*.

It is so satisfying. Better than fish on Friday

Once these fascinating. monologues come to an end it is time to talk about the weather.

"Oh, it's so hot today, I can't do a thing but lie down in front of the TV," says one old person, with a swipe across the forehead to prove a point.

"Oh, I like it hot," says an old person you can count on to be annoying.

"I have never complained about the heat, it's the cold that I hate."

"They said we had a 30% chance of rain yesterday," says another old person in the group.

"Nothing happened, of course. Those meteorologists, or whatever they call themselves, just toss a coin and 50% of the time they're wrong."

Old person number one always has to get the last word.

"I just wet my finger and stick it out the front door to see if the wind is blowing," he says.

Ha! Ha! Ha!

And so it goes on for another half an hour or so.

Then it is time for a nice glass of iced tea on the covered deck. Lots of ice. Then the iced tea competition begins and we have to hear all about how all the other old people make their surely prize-worthy iced-tea.

Oh, the life of the over 60s. You just can't beat it.

What will you wear when you get older?

I have already gotten older, and I can tell you that no matter what I wear I always look pathetic, or worse. My mother used to say that people of a certain age look like *"mutton dressed as lamb,"* if they tried to dress like their daughters, or heaven forbid their granddaughters. I can see now that she was right.

When I reached the tender age of 40, I peered in the mirror and was amazed to see that I didn't have a single wrinkle on my face - no crow's feet, no turkey neck, **no animal parts at all**. I also had nice perky boobs that had no hint of a wrinkly cleavage between them.

Then, heh, a year later when I was 41 that same mirror really let me down. I suddenly noticed a whole crop of wiggly lines branching out in all directions like a complicated road map all over my face. Even my jaw line was no longer smooth, but was interrupted by an ugly bump on either side. Not a pretty sight.

I realized at 50 my full-length mirror was not my friend at all. My knees looked all wobbly and knobbly in short skirts, so I had to wear jeans after that.

Then at 60, real horrors, I noticed that the tops of my arms suddenly looked like *empty suit cases hanging down and wobbling* if I shrugged my shoulders. That was the end of short sleeves. No more short sleeve tee shirts for Sally, and certainly no tank tops either. I would have died of shame if someone had spotted my suit cases wobbling.

Then at 70 all hell broke loose. I can no longer wear short skirts, or short sleeve tee shirts, and seeing as my boobs have definitely gone south, and my stomach sticks out three inches further than my boobs, I just don't go out in daylight hours at all.

I skulk about in hooded robes after dark.

Where can old people go when they go down in size?

There are quite a few places that would be accessible to old people if they really went down in size, although many do not want to take the trouble. If an old person can go down a lot they can go anywhere they like.

They can even have a barrel of fun in the process.

Imagine if an old person was really slim and supple (must be supple) they could make a nice slim Santa and slide down somebody's chimney into their living room.

Ta da!

They must be sure to cut at least two feet off the sides of their red pants first so they don't get stuck half way down. And they mustn't make a lot of noise as it's not nice for the neighbors.

If an old person really slimmed down they could pose as a Genie and grant people's wishes in the supermarket.

They could squeeze into a tiny gap near the meat counter and jump out at people while they are doing their grocery shopping.

Boo!

But they would have to make sure there is no chance of getting their wand bent in the meat grinder as that would make it ineffective.

If they really go down in size, old people can play with the kids for hours. I have seen some skinny old people sailing by in cardboard boxes on the kid's slides.

Whee!

They have a whale of a time. If you want a cheap babysitter take a really skinny old person to the swings and give them a cardboard box to sit in. They can entertain the kids for hours.

Oh, what fun you can have when you go down in size. Can't beat it.

Why can't old people find their words?

Old people cannot find their words because they forget where they have put them. So much for the memory. That goes as well when you get old. So you have a double whammy when it comes to keeping tabs on your words.

Putting your words in a safe place is no good at all if you forget where the safe place is. Old people have safe places all over the house and they have all kinds of words stashed away in them. Some of the words are pretty useless, though, so it doesn't really matter that they can't find them. Imagine fussing over useless words like:

Cat

Dog

Flea

Bug

Yet that's the kind of words that old people are always looking for in safe places. Sometimes they find the cat or the dog curled up in a safe place, surrounded by a lot of stupid old words like *Flea* and *Bug*. The trick is to find the cat and the dog first before they find the *Flea* and the *Bug*. The cat and the dog would not do at all well if they were in a safe place with all the stupid words like *Flea* and *Bug*.

The best thing old people can do is to hang on to the best letters like *X*, *W* and *Q* that are pretty good letters, if you know what to do with them. They can make all kinds of lovely, juicy words that everybody will be jealous of:

Quixotic

Maximize

Wheezily

Jezabel

These words are great for old people because they get them over 75 points each. Who wouldn't want words like that? Old people never lose words like that because they keep them in their pocket. These are called pocket-words. Not to be confused with pocket dogs who are bigger. Sometimes the cat and the dog think they are pocket pets. But old people don't usually have large enough pockets to keep cats and dogs in them.

The best thing they can do is to write down where all the safe places in the house are so that they cannot lose their words. They must always remember where they put the piece of paper with all the best words on them or they will be stuttering all day.

Why do people never seem happy when I talk about my life getting better and better?

You have just discovered a new game. It is called *Ain't it Awful?*

People in groups always play games. They don't know they are playing games, of course, and they don't realize that they only play games with people who will have a hand as good as theirs.

But if you find a good group you can have a truly amazing game that can go on until the wee small hours of the morning. It is so absorbing.

Ain't it Awful? is a very popular game indeed as nearly everyone has something to moan about. And the fact that everybody else in the group hangs onto your every word it is very satisfying.

When a group decides to play a quick hand of **_Ain't it Awful?_** it can be about anything. Let's say, you are the first to play your hand, you might begin the game by saying,

o *"Oh, guess what! My Glenda caught her husband in bed with another woman the other day,"* to which everybody gasps and says,

o *"Oh, no, ain't it awful?"*

o Then the next player plays his hand and says, *"That's nothin', my boy Bill caught his missus in a threesome with two rednecks the other night,"* to which everybody replies:

o *"Oh, no, ain't it awful?"*

And the game heats up. Some games get so steamy you have to get up and open a window, but nothing will stop the game. It can go on all night.

Just so long as you have something really juicy to moan about, you can play the game.

Now here comes **_Mr. Smart Ass_**. He bounds over to where the group is thickly immersed in their game of **_Ain't it Awful?_**, rubs his hands together with glee, throws his head back, and says in his loudest voice:

o *"Guess what! I just won the lottery, and me and the missus is going on a trip to Bali next week."*

Plonk!

Drinks over, glasses down, everybody in the group gets up and walks away leaving *Mr. Smart Ass* talking to himself.

That's why nobody likes a smart ass.

Why do so many websites insist on using gray print? Do they hate seniors?

All websites hate seniors.

And can you blame them? Old people don't have the sense to stick to one website. Instead they keep dodging about from website to website and annoying the website designers.

Websites should be chosen very carefully, and stuck to at all costs. But old people are cantankerous and refuse to stick to anything, least of all websites.

They are just annoying website designers for the fun of it. They should be banned from using computers altogether then they wouldn't be able to keep website hopping all night long and annoying website designers.

Why is it hard for old people to change?

What makes you think it's hard for old people to change?

I'm in my 70s and don't think it is hard to change at all. I do it every day. Or perhaps I should say, I do it whenever I feel the need to change.

Sometimes I wear the same clothes twice, but that is unusual. Most of the time I change my clothes every day.

I have to admit that I find it harder to change these days now that I have a bad arm. I have such a bad arm that I would dearly love to unscrew it and take it off. Or I might just send it back to where it came from. Who knows where arms come from anyway? And legs come to that.

If I was honest, I would say that my bad leg causes me a lot of trouble and I always have a hard time changing my pants. When you have a bad arm and a bad leg you are at a disadvantage. Other people just take their good arms and legs for granted.

Only centipedes should take their legs for granted because they have a lot of them. And only apes should take their arms for granted because they have long arms and can swing from tree to tree. I would love to swing from tree to tree, but I've got a bad arm.

Come to think of it, I also have a bad hand. My hand is so bad that I can't pull my socks on. I have had to go without socks now for years because of my bad hand. I have a pile of socks moldering in the drawer. If you ever need a pair of *moldy socks*, I have just the thing for you – in all colors.

Oh, and I forgot, my bad foot causes me a lot of bother too. The foot that has the sock that won't go on because of the hand that won't work is a big problem for me, and I can't see it ever getting any better.

Sometimes I just think I will stay in bed all day because of my bad arm and my bad leg and my bad hand and my bad foot.

So perhaps you are right after all. Old people do find it hard to change.

Thank you very much for reading this book.
I would really appreciate it if you could leave
me a review on Amazon. Reviews help other
people decide whether or not to read the book.

Thank you so much.

Sally.

About the author

Sally Alter is the author of ten fiction and non-fiction books. She has written extensively on bipolar disorder, has a book on loneliness, a memoir, a book of poetry, 3 novellas in the Shards of Glass series, and a short story One Summer. She is presently working on "After the Suicide," a memoir of photographs. She also writes for Quora and has 47 million views and a following of 19,000 people.

She was born in London, but currently lives in Texas with her cat Greta. She paints in oils and makes collages in her spare time.

Facebook: @ SallyAlterWriter
Website: sallyalter.com

Her credentials include: being the past editor of Illuminations—Schreiner University's International e-journal. Her poetry has been widely published in Illuminations, The Muse, The Texas Poetry Calendar, Houston Poetry Anthology, Austin International Poetry Anthology, The Kerrville Daily Times and The Hill Country Community Journal.

Her books include (c.Oct 2024):

FICTION

Shards of Glass Series
Shards of Glass
Fragments of the Past
Memories Lost in Time

SHORT STORIES

One Summer

NON FICTION

How to Live with Bipolar
Bipolar 1 Disorder Rescue Plan
37 Symptoms of Bipolar Depression
The Bipolar Guide
A Practical Guide to Overcoming Loneliness

POETRY

We Never Did Mornings

HUMOUR

Funny Old Folk